T0268706

THE MANY HUNDREDS OF THE SCENT

THE MANY HUNDREDS
OF THE SCENT

SHANE McCRAE

FARRAR STRAUS GIROUX / NEW YORK

Farrar, Straus and Giroux
120 Broadway, New York 10271

Photograph on title spread and page 69: *Brixton Riot, 1981*,
by Neil Libbert / Bridgeman Images.

The Library of Congress has cataloged the hardcover edition as follows:
Names: McCrae, Shane, 1975– author.
Title: The many hundreds of the scent : poems / Shane McCrae.
Description: First edition. | New York : Farrar, Straus and Giroux, 2023.
Identifiers: LCCN 2022043725 | ISBN 9780374607197 (hardcover)
Subjects: LCGFT: Poetry.
Classification: LCC PS3613.C385747 M36 2023 | DDC 811/.6—dc23/eng/20220912
LC record available at https://lccn.loc.gov/2022043725

Paperback ISBN: 978-0-374-61394-5

Designed by Crisis

Our books may be purchased in bulk for promotional, educational,
or business use. Please contact your local bookseller or the Macmillan
Corporate and Premium Sales Department at 1-800-221-7945, extension
5442, or by email at MacmillanSpecialMarkets@macmillan.com.

www.fsgbooks.com
Follow us on social media at @fsgbooks

10 9 8 7 6 5 4 3 2 1

That rocked thee like a cradle to thy root   —JOHN CLARE

CONTENTS

THE MANY HUNDREDS OF THE SCENT

THE MANY HUNDREDS
OF THE SCENT

Friend, I have turned   the brambles back. I used
    An instrument, a weapon, though it wasn't
    A weapon, it was an instrument, an oar
To which I had affixed a sheet of plywood
    Three feet by three feet,   earlier, an instrument
    A weapon,   something like a sword with
A large square tip, but like a sign
    A protester might wave.   I leaned the plywood
    Against the brambles as I walked the path
This morning, leaning   all my weight against the plywood
    Repeatedly, so that I must have looked
    Like a pro wrestler as I turned the brambles
This morning, bouncing off the ropes,   but end-
    less ropes at the single boundary of an endless
    Ring,   though it isn't endless, the path ends
But who was watching me   this morning as I walked the clotted
    Path, breaking sorrows from the path
    Follow the path. I've yet to sweep the wreckage
Of the brambles from its edges.   You will find
    The tower we have often built together
    You from imagination, I from memory

As beams of the last sunlight blurri-
  ly flared across the wall, the last of the day, shaped by the blinds
  Each glowing on the wall as if each beam were
A ghost   beam of wood floating from the wall
  Burning.   And we have watched as slowly
  They flew away   into the dark
And though we know it's an illusion made by
  The sunlight through the blinds, the slats are shaped
  Like beams of wood, the spaces where they don't fit
Together, shaped like beams of wood
  Through which the sunlight enters, still we
  Have watched the beams that hold the house together flee the wall
Like ashes flying   upward, burning
  Didn't you once confide in me
  You stumbled chasing ashes with your eyes as
The ashes fled a fire you couldn't yet
  See clearly   raging in the heart of the copse you
  Had been approaching,   as they rose above the tops
Of the tallest of the band of ever-
  greens, and the ashes   might have been pine needles flying from
  The pines, but   none of the trees, no pine, no cedar
No fir tree burned, you heard no noise
  Of burning,   but you felt the heat, and you had
  Seen light?   No telling what had called
You to the window. Was it   merely that you wanted
  To see the snow?   You saw the distant light
  Of the fire burning in the copse beyond the barn, and

You realized you might not ever have

    Another chance to see the trees up close whose

    Provenance and continued health, exposed

To storms of black exhaust and storms of gravel

    Kicked from the gravel road by pickup trucks

    As the trucks fishtail past the gate   and the copse marking

The limit of my property

    Had, from the day you   first appeared and spoke to

    Me, seemed incomprehensible to you

What did you say then,   not your first words

    To me, but those you whispered as I turned the locks

    Curious who had struck the door so fiercely

So frantically had rung the doorbell? It

    Had been,   but I was young,   a child still

    Ten years since any visitor had come unasked

And you so calm on the porch, not even

    Facing the door.   I thought for sure you were

    Watching whoever had knocked, had rung, was running

Away,   but there was no one there but you

    And as you neared the copse, when you were twenty

    Ten feet away, the trees seemed suddenly

To huddle closer to the burning center

    As if they were protecting it

    And just as suddenly you turned and ran back

To the house.   No strangeness mars the path

    Now, friend.   I've turned back even

    The strangeness that once made the path

Familiar, and the trees by standing still, by moving
    Only with the wind, will answer your old fear
    And curiosity,   and at the end of the path you
Will see the tower,   distant still, but rising, at
    First by itself against the sky, but soon you
    Will see the fruiting orange grove, the leaves
Of the tallest trees obscuring from your vision
    The tower's lowest windows. You
    Will know at once it is no fearful
And burning heart, the tower, the low-
    est windows of which you do not yet see. Amidst the orange
    Trees, their suspended   flames, you'll find
A peaceful place,   my memories of which I've
    Until now guarded by allowing dense
    Brambles to overgrow the only path to the orange
Grove.   But I've turned them back, the brambles, with
    An instrument, a weapon.   Take the path.   Before you
    Can see the grove you will   smell it, a ghost
Of oranges in the air. One ghost   of oranges is
    Hundreds of ghosts, a lifetime each, of each
    The many hundreds of the scent   of oranges you've tasted
Newborn each time you tasted it, that hung
    Like rain on the air, that for so long as
    It hangs on the air makes air the purest form of rain
The tower will seem to rise from the scent it-
    self, from the scent of oranges
    In the midst of the   undifferentiated view, as

If scent, like touch, were place,   a home not made
    Of memories, but the next, searching inhalation
    Always the next, with which the scent returns

RACE IN THE BODY

To live and not   to understand
My body, who it lives. To live
Allowed   the black of the blackness of
    The back of my black hand

A gift   of the back of my own hand
Upon which I can balance things
But can't hold them,   and not the pink
    Of the black palm I hold

Now toward you, now toward you
And almost   it's your own outstretched
Hand in a perfect darkness, which
    You now can't place, can't know

In the perfect darkness   in the un-
familiar room.   The feeling you
Can't   place your hand,   that's really you
    Not knowing how the room

Is furnished, will   you stumble over
The heart of the room, a thing   so low, if
You hadn't gone the way you're going
     You would have passed forever

Over it, your hand forever   float-
ing in an atmosphere above
The possibility of touch-
     ing   that which, were you not

A stranger here, could only seem
Strange if you looked at it too long
A low or   in a corner thing
     That makes the room the room

It is, the   bed, the television
Or the long, shrouded desk, upon
Which once, but how could you have known
     A neighbor laid a twitching

Animal, broken, sticky with
Blood, nobody would   say it was blood
Except out loud, nobody inside
     Themselves,   instead they shout-

ed it, their   panic carrying
The blood away, each shout the body
Of the word,   *Blood!*   neighbor and children
     And parent, someone brings

Paper towels and a cup
Of water from the kitchen, later
No one remembers who, tap   water
    Whoever it was stopped

To choose a ruined cup,   from the back
Of the cabinet, the   children clean
Their brushes in it, when they paint
    Stained water   pales the dark

Blood as the shuddering animal
Dies, from which cup   only a stranger
Would drink.   Where is the heart?   With the lights on
    You see no stain at all

THE PHANTOM SON

Each surface, every   surface is   a mirror as
Much as it is a wall.   I do not see myself
In any surface.   But that's how I know myself
That I'm invisible.   I do not hear my voice

Echoing like   I hear the voices of my mother
My father and my sister echoing, the soft
Vibrations I don't think they feel   with each word soft-
ly passing through them, broken by the walls, each other

Their bodies and the furniture,   but not my bod-
y, phantom,   each word crumbling as it touches them
Not sped by me to silence, passing through. To them
Alone I speak as if I speaking might be heard

Might be for speaking touched, all day, and as I fall
Asleep,   my thoughts decaying like a sound in air
Until what I say makes no sense, and the cool air
The susurrations in it, overcomes me, all

The silences of the dimmed house   and all the sounds
Of sleeping in it clashing, neither meshing with
The other, carry me   to sleep. I am most with
My family then, each of us dreaming, each unknown

READING IS ON YOUR
LIST OF CHORES

The world is wild and sad, you're wild and sad
Daughter, and you want only,   but you on-
ly want   to watch the videos you want
To watch, the worlds you want to see,   to be allowed

To not be   told the world
Is none of the worlds you're watching, none
Of the any worlds that would allow   at an-
y moment you to rise and walk away, is none of the worlds you could

Turn from, your head away, by
Leaving it tame it, though it takes its wildness from your fear
And we have told you No
And we have told you   to stay here
And read, that we   will help you understand here, from which you
    can't go
That understanding is not taming

RACE IN LANGUAGE

Look back   a generation, I look back
    Ten generations on my mother's side
Further, to England and to Ireland
    Knowing ten words they knew, a thousand words

Knowing the language they, my ancestors
    Knew on my mother's side, in Ireland
In England. I look back   two genera-
    tions on my father's side, his mother and

His father, and I'm sure I know them, most
    Of the words they knew. I can't look back and know
Their fathers or their mothers.   I can guess
    Six generations back,   or seven, too

Many far back past   seven, back   at eight or
    Further, I might not, if I stood before them
Any   who lived in Africa, I might
    Not know a single word.   What could I say

What object could I,   if I stood before
 Them, any ancestor,   what object could
I gesture to, to   start to learn the language
 Wherever I have met them, if I stood

Before them,   any one, if there were trees
 There, I could touch a tree, say   *Tree*, then point
To them, then back to the tree,   or thump my chest
 And say my name, or say *You are my aunt*

Or say *You are my father many fathers*
 Before him.   What are we?   What is your word
For you?   What do you know about the ocean
 If he lived inland.   If he lived beside

The ocean, if   whatever carried me
 Through time to him   could keep us there forever
I could stand listening forever, between
 Him and the ocean.   I could stand forever

O D E

A cup from the shelf, cup from behind the measur-
ing cup, a blue cup   from when Eden was
A toddler, a child's   cup, who held the cup
In two hands like a grown-up holding hot
Cocoa, a cup from the shelf, behind the measuring
Cup, itself glass and perfectly transparent, ex-
cept for the lines and numbers, red
Lines and red numbers,   through which no light passes
Without which, it, the measuring
Cup is a pouring cup, a handle and a spout
No other use for it if parts of it
Didn't obstruct the gaze with its
Familiar information, and a filling cup
Same use, two   ounces, then four ounces, then
Six ounces, then a cup,   and then a final
Inch,   toward which   the cup has seemed
The whole   climb of its body to aspire
Of unmarked glass, the blank that meets the high
Unmeasure of its course, a filling cup
A pouring cup, a handle and a spout

A beak, a lip, no   name I know, half spout, half beak
Whole lip, the top half,   if it were a spout
A beak, shorn off, no need for, if
It were a mouth, another half to make it whole
The human mouth in parts
Each dignified, each named as if it were a whole
A lip, a tooth, a tongue, a cup from the shelf
Cerulean,   too big for her to
Hold with one hand when   she was small enough to
Be satisfied by what the cup could hold
So held it as if she were savoring
Hot cocoa, and imagining herself
In far another country, at
A café at a table on the sidewalk
Wearing, perhaps, a frayed red scarf
And effortful ensemble, calculated to
Appear to anybody native to the city
Casual, native to the city
And so to be the stage for the surprise
Of the native to the city when her slight
But unmistakably American
Accent is heard, as she responds
To the inquiry about, say, local politics
With which she was approached   by the native to the city
And so she set her cocoa down and spoke
A cup   from the shelf, cerulean
Frosted like frosted glass, though plastic, a

Clouded clear ocean, ocean mixed with sand
Kicked from the ocean floor, an ocean at a shore
Pulled down   and filled with punch made
From fruits I can't imagine making
The flavor they have made, blue with small dying clouds
Rising and falling just beneath the thrashing surface,   a small patch
Of thrashing, small   white clouds, that seem to rise
Though they are dying, eagerly to rise
To meet the running child creating them

THE DOORWAY

Dido stood   at the tide line
Watching Aeneas's ship
Burn on the horizon, a

Small sand-colored dog nibbling
At her ankle.   Though Carthage
Itself had seemed to whisper

For days of her shamelessness
With Aeneas, the city
Breathing without her   even

As she at last felt she filled
The city, she had not blushed
When a priest whispered the news

Of Aeneas's sudden
Flight in her ear, but only
Waved at the captain behind

Him, who turned and waved at men
Stationed on the other side
Of a doorway, through which, at

That moment, she would not look
Now, she pictured Aeneas
Wildly swinging his bright sword

Panicked, killing his own men
His son weeping, whose fragile
Body had lured her into

Aeneas's arms.   She saw
Aeneas bloodied, with a
Carthaginian arrow

Through his neck, his arms spread wide
Floating,   for a moment, face-
down in the sea, before his

Heavy armor buried him
She clapped her hands together
And the dog sat suddenly

Upright, trained to expect meat
At the sound,   but she had none
He barked, and she clapped again

SOMETHING GRAND I WAS

We must have flown, I don't remember flying
My mother's parents, me a three-year-old
We must have flown. We couldn't have if who
Was going   to drive the car from Oregon
To Texas, Salem, that means peace,   to Austin
He was a soldier, Steve F. Austin

I see us sometimes in a C-130
A military plane, but big enough
For us, our car and things from Oregon
To Texas, Salem, that means peace,   too big
For us, our car and things, but shouldn't it
Have been too big, enormous, something grand

I was   being kidnapped, shouldn't it have been
Impossible? One hundred thousand pounds
Of steel, aluminum, and blood, the sky
Itself incredulous and mocking?   Shouldn't
A flock of birds have struck the props like laughter
Shouldn't the sky have laughed us from its bursting heart

IN THE DITCH WHERE THE CAMERA FINDS MY BODY

I'm splashing in the driveway in a ditch
In which a corpse of rain has gathered, here
A corpse has gathered,   wearing noth-
ing, a full diaper. I am three.   A clear

Sky leans as if upon a bar upon
The house and everyone in the picture, my
Grandmother, me. I am   the rain come down
My mother's parents have just kidnapped me

I am the corpse in which I play. I'm danc-
ing in the corpse.   The clear sky sickens
Watching, but with   no clouds in the sky the sky can't move

Away.   Behind me, picking
Flowers my mother's mother sees   the green has fled the leaf
O reader,   listener, stay.   You are now evidence

AFTER MY GRANDPARENTS KIDNAP ME THEY MOVE TO A NEW DEVELOPMENT

The only scenes I know are scenes
My mother's parents thought to take
Pictures of. Me in the ditch,   my mother's father
        In the yard before the fence

Was built, before the lawn was fit
-ted to the Earth's   face like a face
After a mauling.   He is posing like
        A hunter in the dirt

He grips a hoe and kneels in the corpse
Called *Everywhere.*   A neighborhood
Is coming.   Where an armed man kneels and grins
        That man will build a house

FAR PAST THE END

After the first few months or after how
-ever long, after   they my mother's parents
Stopped taking   pictures of me looking happy
As if against the day

They would need pictures of me looking happy
To get a lighter sentence,   I remember
Nothing of what in the first months after happened
But still I must have been

Dying, I had been   taken from my life
My life I don't   remember once remembering
Still I was   three and I   must have been happy
Sometimes, and even with them

My mother's parents, who had kidnapped me
Dying but sometimes hungry, sleepy
Sometimes, and even when   I missed my father, must have
Wanted to play, even when

I still remembered what he looked like, what his
Voice sounded like.   How happy must you keep the
Child you have kidnapped if you want
Him to forget?   or clap

How loud each time he turns his head to look
At something you can't see   in the doorway? How
Far past the end of the old life is the end
Of the living memory

SEAGULLS CRYING

To the beach at where,   at anywhere a beach is
But might have been   in Oregon, unless my
Grandparents were afraid   I would be known there
My kidnapping,   or there I would remember they
        Had kidnapped me, and say

So to a stranger, so, and so, and so, and
At whom and for how long then would they have to
Smile to get free, how   whitely nod and wriggle
To keep their black   pet? Smile at whom, how far beneath
        Them,   the last smile on Earth

Or to the beach at the Gulf of Mexico, some
Several fewer thousand miles from Austin
And where the water looked unnatural colored
To me who hadn't then before   seen water not
        Bound on all sides, penned,   caught

And blue, kept   clean the influx there prevented
Of influence from other waters,   said to

But said by whom who weren't themselves corrupted
Said to be water just the same as that which e-
      ven I, a child, could see

Looked clean being blue, a child,   but taught to value
Purity.   I was four,   was five, was six, that
Child a hallucination now.   My mother's
Parents, it was summer, took me there.   And almost none
      Of it, most of it gone

Now,   I remember almost none of it, not
Even myself, a dream now, I remember
Except the crying seagulls at the window
Of the hotel room in which we stayed, from which I don't
      Remember leaving once

Except to go back home, the crying seagulls
Crying at our window, at   no other crying
Until I threw them bread. My mother's mother
Had packed a loaf of bread.   I tore the loaf apart
      As fast as I could tear

It, each   brown slice apart,   and threw the pieces
To the seagulls. Who   is standing next to me, which
Kidnapper,   smiling,   a hallucination
Helping with the loaf,   but will not let me leave the room
      Not even leave with them

Not hand in hand with them, down to the water
To watch the seagulls there, that might not cry so
Hungrily there?   And some would hover quiet
Above the waves,   and some would settle on the waves
And none would know my face

EXPLAINING MY APPEARANCE
IN CERTAIN PICTURES

In pictures now I do not smile and didn't
Then, I would laugh if I was being tickled
And sometimes one, my mother's mother would tick-
le me, and the   other would take the picture
My mother's father, and so sometimes I'm
Not smiling but I'm laughing, my eyes closed
And my mouth open, almost like I'm scream-
ing, but I'm laughing,   when I was a child

In pictures with my kidnappers, with one
My mother's mother always her.   I'm sitting
Most often in her lap, her arms around
My blurred   waist, she has me on Rita-
lin, and the trick   is wait until
The laughing stops.   As the mouth closes you can take the smile

IN THE HOUSE FROM WHICH
I WAS KIDNAPPED

The pale blinds rise and fall, a gif forever
The blinds move   on their own.   At first my father
Stands with the string between his fingers, first
And middle, pulling, even   after it tears
Into his fingers, tears the first and mid-
dle skin,   him pulling, letting go, his blood
Staining the length of the looped string near-
est him.   He pulls the string for years

Eventually he backs   away from the window
Into the room.   He doesn't turn.   Now
He watches from a shadow in the room
For a small child to be returned to him
I see him watching from   deeper in the shadow
Whenever I look   into his eyes.   The shadow grows the way a
    child grows

I HAVE MIXED MY LABOR
WITH THE SOIL

Back at the old house, the woods, no entry now
How much remains if any of my blood
And skin in the forest up the hill?   Unend-
ing the humiliations so small you
Can't talk about them or they stop being true
Such as sound loyal in your head
And do betray you on your tongue.   It is my bod-
y still,   more mine than when how long ago
I bled at war in the woods with boys I wanted
To like me so I let them hurt me there
I wore a helmet from the army surplus store
Hoping I would be hunted
And shot in the head, hoping I'd hear the BB strike
To squeeze through brambles my own blood made thick

MY MOTHER WAS A DANCER

I danced with the boy in the yard, my mother watching us
    He held his left hand high, but too far back
      As if it had been photographed mid-wave
        And frozen by the attentive flash

As if he once had   meant to swing it down, and now
    Couldn't, a fear   I knew and couldn't name
      For years, but bodied by my mother's gaze
        Gripped it, and wouldn't let it go

He turned to her,   and, crying, shouted wasn't she
    Going to do anything? My mother's   teeth
      Parted. But what she said I didn't hear
        Again I struck his bleeding eye

HELEN

1. HELEN'S SPEAR

Helen studied Achilles
From her room in the palace
That was Paris's room while

Paris fretted and paced, or
Slept, or bragged to his pages
About the swiftness with which

He would dispatch Achilles
If only his father would
Allow him to fight.   "The life

Of a prince   is not his own"
He would say to the three bored
Boys, and to the fourth boy, who

Listened,   "He owes his duty
Not to the great, no, lads, but
To the humble,"   and he would

Turn then   to the window from
Which Helen watched Achilles
Kill, but he would close his eyes

Helen studied Achilles
Helen   studied him as she
Had studied her furious

Husband, Menelaus, in
The months before she fled him
With Paris.   Helen studied

Achilles, memorizing
Him, this   small, quick man, who was
More fearsome than her husband

Within a year, whenever
She saw him knock a spear thrust
Away, she felt his muscles

Twitch beneath her skin, she leaped
Back   whenever a Trojan
Lunged at him, and in the years

That followed, she began to
Lunge at him, she began to
Knock his spear away.   And soon

She realized her lunges
Were faster than his, her spear
Was faster, and as she and

Paris watched Hector emerge
From the city   to battle
Achilles for the first time

She said to Paris, "I love
Your brother, but Achilles
Will kill him, and your father

Will command you then   to fight
Achilles.   Command your boys
To prepare your armor, but

Not the youngest. I don't think
The child could bear to lose you"
Paris nodded, and that night

While Helen pretended to
Sleep, escaped   the palace through
The secret tunnel she had

Mentioned to the youngest page
The day before.   Helen rose
And stepped to the window.   She

Watched Paris sneak from shadow
To shadow   across the beach
Her spear arm twitched as she watched

The voice of Achilles rolled
Over the gates, and many
In the city thought the gates
Had been breached, so loudly did

His voice resound.   And some men
Fell immediately, as
If they had been commanded
On their swords, abandoning

Their children, their wives, their slaves
To the wrath they heard coming
The wrath   was one man, making
Himself look taller, a few

Inches, his voice sound slightly
Louder, by standing on his
Toes   on the back of the corpse
Of the warrior he had

Fought and killed the day before
Hector, once the champion
Of Troy, before the city's
Unbroken gates and high walls

He shouted, "The best of you
By far is now dead. Return
The wife of Menelaus
And I will spare your city

Defy me, and I will claim
Your wives." And some men heard this
And thought he spoke from their homes
Their beds, and fell on their swords

In the palace, Helen stepped
Away from her window, and
Strapped on Paris's armor
And the bronze mask he wore when

Sparring,   though his opponents
Fearing execution, had
Always avoided his face
Took his spear and his thick shield

And snuck from the palace   through
The tunnel through which Paris
Had escaped the night before
Emerging   on the other

Side of the wall a hundred
Feet from Achilles.   She made
her voice deep, and she shouted
"I am Paris, prince of Troy

I come now to kill the man
Who killed my brother."   Helen
Didn't wait for Achilles
To reply, but ran toward

Him, sunlight glaring off the
Mask, changing its aspect from
Paris's playful glower
To the face of Thanatos

Not smiling and not frowning
Who doesn't fight, but reaps.   She
Rammed Achilles from Hector's
Back   with her heavy shield, and

Almost knocked him down, but he
Stumbled backward into Greeks
Who shoved him forward again
He pulled his spear from the sand

Where he had left it erect
Next to Hector's corpse, and lunged
At Helen, who knocked the tip
Of his spear down with her spear

And his spear lodged in the sand
And raised Achilles for a
Moment   like a vaulting pole
For a long moment   he held

The spear, and the awed Greeks watched
Him rise,   but then he let go
And landed square on his feet
Achilles cried out   for a

Spear, and Odysseus flung
Hector's spear to him.   He caught
It as he leaped at Helen
Slamming his shield into hers

Breaking her shield arm, though she
Didn't feel it breaking, but
Only slid   backward in the
Sand a few inches, and raised

Her spear to block the hacking
Strike Achilles attempted
With Hector's spear.   Hector's spear
Weakened in the fight between

Hector and Achilles, broke
On Helen's spear, and Helen
Kicked Achilles's legs from
Beneath him, and flung away

Her spear. She   jumped on him then
Pinning his arms with her knees
And smashed the edge of her shield
Down on his face, just above

His nose, and smashed the edge of
Her shield   down on his throat, and
Smashed the edge of her shield down
On his forehead, and as she

Raised her shield to smash it down
Again, she saw blood dripping
From the edge, and shards of bone
As dark as blood, falling from

The iron edge of her shield
And she turned and smashed the edge
Of her shield down on his groin
And she stood, and threw her shield

At the backs of the Greeks, who
Were fleeing now to their ships
Some men in the city still
Groaned, their swords in their stomachs

Paris's pages, who had
Never once attended him
In battle, left the city
To claim Hector's corpse for Troy

3. HELEN AFTER TROY

The battle over, Helen
Raised her mask.   Blood dimmed its bronze

Cheeks and forehead, its bronze chin
Shielded her eyes from the sun

She ordered her youngest page
Who had before served Paris

To hurry back to Troy, and
To return with Hector's horse

To lead the horse on a new
Rope to her.   And though the horse

Refused   to trample the smashed
Corpse of Achilles into

The sand he had earned, still she
Untied it, first feeling then

Her shield arm was broken,   still
She shouted the horse away

PENELOPE AND THE
WATCHING FIRE

She burned the loom each
Night, for heat. But each
Morning it returned

Whole, and draped with a
Restless blue fabric
A wave's skeleton

The first few mornings
It appeared, she was
Surprised by the wave

She had publicly
Vowed she would not lay
Eyes upon the sea

Until her husband
Who even as she
Spoke her vow, perhaps

Lay drowned in the sea
Returned. And soon, she
Came to believe the

Wave was sent to her
By the god of waves
To torment her. One

Of her suitors, an
Attractive man, but
Too young, had told her

As her husband's slaves
Cleared breakfast from the
Room, of the blinding

Of the Cyclops by
No Man, who she was
Sure was her husband

Perhaps the bones with
Which she wove were his
Perhaps she would not

See him again, but
Instead would labor
Always, her fingers

Bloodying the blue
Threads, at the machine
Of her husband's bones

And so, she thought of
Him, long years into
His absence, as his

Slaves stuffed the loom, its
Hollow parts, the gaps
In its workings, with

Straw, as she watched them
Bend, who could not choose
How to use their strength

THE FUNGUS CALLED
DEAD MAN'S FINGERS

It's true, the fungus does look like a dead man's fingers
Look   at a picture of the fungus if you don't believe
Me, or a dead   woman's, it's true, if how we think
The dead man died was he was murdered, and he reaches

From the heart of the earth imploring,   or it might as well be
The heart of the earth, six   feet below the surface, for
How clear the grave is when I try to picture it
How clear the heart where men lie   is, if he was killed

By love, once love, said   it was love, not
The love that packed the body in the heart of the earth, not
The last   love, that informed or instigated the concern
To see the body buried, to see the gray cheeks blushed

Before the grave winch married it to the earth, not
The love at the beginning of the chain of un
-doing being, love waving   at itself and us, of the chain of not
Revivifying, but   of gesturing toward life, a burying

Love, but a love that hides   in the crowd at the funeral, its face
Small, like the face of a boy, cross-armed, sitting in
A plastic chair in the hall outside the murmuring
Door   with the boy who punched him, small   but powerfully

Alone now,   how a boy will use his wound
To make his way in the world, like an impossible
Omnidirectional red carpet now unfurling
Backward through time, from the theater to the limo, from

His future loves to his eye swollen shut
If we imagine it was love that killed the dead man
Said it was love,   whose fingers reach from the heart of the earth
Toward you, the dead man is a woman and you know her

YOUR BLACK CHILD

America you never had a black child
I tell myself you never had a black child
America because I love you still
Because I have to love you, since you're still
Alive.   But how are you alive
When your black child is dead, who was alive
And you were   every moment of her life
Watching her close,   who should have been your life

I tell myself America she was
Your life. I tell myself you knew she was
Because I have to love you still, since you
Are still   alive, and it's a day since you
Killed her—   because I am your black child
I raise my hands from the keys   slowly   because I am your black child

CONSTRUCTION WORKERS
AT NIGHT

Two workers, one on either side of the hole, pull
    The ladder through. The hole is square, two
  Feet by two feet, one story off the ground
Cut in a fence between two buildings.   They are there to

Make sure the ladder doesn't slip and vanish
    Into the darkness past the blinking
  Edge of the light cast   by the caged bulb, where hell
Has sometimes been,   to feed the ladder to the thin king

Who eats the world. They do not watch the hole
    They do not watch the worker who
  Hands up the silvery ladder, but the ladder
Itself, the gleam it bears   from the light it passes through

THE STAGGERING MAN

after Bill Traylor's untitled drawing commonly known as
Man Carrying Dog on Object

I wear the anvil and the dog
I carry them, the dog atop
The anvil.   You might think the an-
vil a caulked basket, me an African

Carrying water home from the well
The river,   in a basket on
My head.   It is an anvil, cast
Steel, painted blue, like water.   I walked past

The river in a dream once, walked
Along the river, carrying
The anvil.   When I looked and saw
My shadow on the water, where the blue

Anvil, its shadow, should have been
Nothing,   the shadow of the dog
Floating above my head.   I wake
Sweating, afraid,   too eager, and I check

The corner of the still black room
Immediately for my burden
I leap from bed and reach for the anvil
The dog bites through my hand before I can pull

It back, though   I had felt the cold
Pouring from the steel, and the wet heat
Of the dog's breath.   As you can see
I hold a cane in one hand, balance the

Anvil with the other. Now which hand for
Which?   Joy distracted me.   To have
Dreamed such a dream! To have survived it
My burden,   disappeared! But I arrived at

The answer.   With the healthy hand
I keep my burden safe, and with
The cane I hold   in the wounded hand
I punch my dripping blood into the earth

THE SPEECH OF THE

THIN KING'S MINDER

The thin king bound in the fiery hollow shook
The chain by which his left arm was suspended
And from a hatch that rattled open just

Above his right eye dropped a demon like
A glass-winged gerbil, who immediately
Began to stab the thin king's pupil with

A dripping claw, and said, *Forgive me, king*
For my unwilling violence. I bite
My paws off, but they grow back while I chew

So that I wonder while I'm chewing, Is
This still my paw I'm chewing, *and, forgive*
Me, king, but that thought helps me swallow. I

Was just now talking to the cook, I don't
Know this one's name, don't ask me what his name is
He's got a head that looks like, right at the top

A knot in an oak tree. I think he must
Talk through the hole he listens with. I have to
Shout through his voice to talk to him, for all

The who-knows-what he tries to tell me. I
Don't like to stare, so when I talk to him
I perch on the edge of the knot and shout, so I'm

Too close to see the knot. Anyway, I
Was talking, and I had to pull my face
Out of the hole to breathe, and when I did

Forgive me, king. You know I can't stop stabbing
Your eye. You know I have to hold your eyelid
Open whenever you try to blink. You know

I have to hold it open with my teeth
You know I've tried to swallow them. Forgive me
Anyway, when I pulled my head from the knot

I saw a new sign hanging from the line
Above the stove, where the cooks drain the bodies
Hanging between two bodies, on a sinew

And the sign read, You cannot love your mother
And let your neighbor starve. *I saw the sign*
And heard a moaning sound approaching from

The knot, a moaning and a rasping scream
Both sounds approaching me together, and
I looked in the knot and saw what looked like eyes

A pair of eyes, furious, rising from
The darkness in the knot, not glowing, but
Their fury made them visible. I saw

In the eyes fury great as yours once was
Hunger more hollow than you could sustain
Now. They rose fixed on me, and as they rose

I noticed, at first sheathing, and then growing
From my claws, icicles of blood, that grew
Down toward the eyes as quick as the eyes rose

I lost my balance, and I fell from the knot
And almost into the tall flame the cook
Was using to make pancakes, but I stopped

Myself. Hovering there, above the flame
Beneath the knot, I only heard the cook
Humming a song I didn't recognize

Each long note slid across the knot, ice sliding
Across a pond the moment winter leaves it
I turned my head and looked up, and no eyes

Emerged, but each of the bodies on the line
Opened its eyes, but lifelessly, and only
To glance at the icicles now melting into

The batter, then each closed its eyes again
Forgive me, at that moment a thought seized me
And holds me still. If God's your mother—surely

God is your mother, king, who with the first
Made things was made—and loving God would free you
How many must you feed or else despair

The earth has not yet swallowed up so many
I think. I was just shaking my paws dry
And thinking when you rang. And here I am

Blood pearled at the wound in the eye of the thin king
Who eats the world and burns in the hollow center
Of the world. The demon bit the lid and held it

AS IF ITS PRISON

It's going up and coming down most often
I think I'll die.   When the machine
Shakes like a fishhook shakes both as and after
The fish shakes   itself loose and after in-

to the lake again. The fishhook   shakes at the end
Of the shaking line; I watch the shaking hook
Don't watch the leaping   splash. But sometimes even when
The plane has leveled and seems stable.   A mistake

To ever assume calm and safety are
The same thing.   Music shakes the air as if
It wants to escape the air
As if its prison were not keeping it alive

H E X

One's opportunities to be unhappy are
Unlimited.   Or limited, but only by
One's own imagination, which is powerful
But fragile, is defenseless,   but is limited
Only by things unseen.   As Bark Psychosis did it
In music, at the start of the new music, *Hex*
Itself the start of the new music, after Talk
Talk started it, who after This Heat started it
Who after Public Image Limited, though John
Lydon has since gone bad, or more offensively
Is who he always was, who after Public Image
Limited started it, going   bad, and not to mention
Slint, not to mention the Americans, Lydon
And Morrissey gone, for   or in Americans
America, for Trump or in Los Angeles
Bad, Morrissey,   not even new, was never new
Except his talent was, and Johnny Marr's,   and always
The dead old art will suffer further life if new
Artists of irresistible ability
Work to extend it,   though such artists must not seek

To extend the   dead old art, or they will fail, but must
Make only what they must   make, and if it aligns
With the dead, the dead will live again in what they make
Low strings,   and keening dissonances when the strings
Ascend together, sirens of the cops inside
Their wooden bodies, their brown bodies. Listen, first
The sirens come from nowhere in the world except
For them, for them the sirens come, announcing nowhere
And then the lights from nowhere round the corner, red
Like an idea of fire, as the drums roll beneath
The strings, a shopping   cart from far from where it rolls
Beneath the city   on a sidewalk in the day
In the middle of the city, roll beneath the city
The strings from which the sirens come, the lights that chase
The sirens down, and live as an idea of fire
And nowhere no guitars.   But space and stillness where
Guitars would be.   Stillness and space and a boy singing
His lone unhappiness in the midst of the raw world
To whom I would escape   from the midst of the raw world
Its now oppressive stillness,   and its windowless
Disease, its timelessness, its timelessness, its nothing's
Happening in my life,   I don't have time to be
Dead, where   to run from timelessness   in the windowless
Room, in the room   in which you sealed yourself   at the start
Of the pandemic, hoping for more life, more time
As Bark Psychosis did it   at the start of the new
Music, and made a sound to which one wanders from

Life,   and in which one wanders still, having arrived
One's opportunities to be unhappy are
Unlimited, though often lately limited
By the end of the world.   But maybe the end of the world is ending
Maybe soon   one will be in small ways sad again
One's opportunities available to one's
Attention, Lydon's to the horseman whinnying
Himself on the fetid, bloating horse, long since afraid
To kick his spurs and pop it,   but he makes an eager
Whinnying, hoping to sound ready. He is ready
To be the last American, whinny and hex
And whinny, hills unfurl beneath him to the hills
Beneath the surface of Lake Erie and the ice
Above the hills   that seems to constitute the lake
From somewhere other than the lake, to be a picture
Of a dead lake, the surface of the thing a picture
Of something else. How far we travel now to be
In the now impossible   presence of things, to which
We ride in light,   that touches and is never touched
All things, by anything, us, even in the light
How far we travel we have traveled to, to watch
The lake unmoving from the parking lot, approaching
The moment, it, the moment   was already in
Our minds accomplished, the long visionary gaze
Across the ice, in the midst of which, the gaze, the ice
Infinite, has no midst, no middle, but is made
Of middles echoing,   in the midst of the gaze, the moment

Through which, the visionary moment, we will leave

Our bodies, gazing, or at least our minds, for once

Won't trouble what we see, such peace accomplished, we

Have known our peace accomplished   on the drive to the lake

And by the time we reach the lake, we've turned around

Already, in our minds, such peace accomplished and

Retreated from, except we park, except we gaze

At the white expanse, and sigh, not knowing which emotion

Demands the sigh, and the sigh leaves us, staggering

A butterfly, our frozen breath, as butterflies

Have staggered, you have watched them, seemed uncertain where

To land, upon which flower, you've watched a butterfly

Choosing,   or if it wasn't choosing, still it seemed

To choose   a flower patterned like itself, our breath

Escaping in the haze of its occasion, you

Watch yours disintegrate and do not recognize

Yourself.   But I am watching and I see you breathing

And watching   I can't see beneath the picture of

Awe on your face, the image of the visionary

Moment, and even if it isn't happening

Beneath the image, I forgive myself for feeling

Nothing, no visionary moment, seeing yours

And the hills roll beneath the surface of the lake

As Mogwai did it, no   singing but in guitars

And sometimes human voices singing, keyboards sometimes

In 1997, three years after *Hex*

At the start of the new music, each guitar a wall

And hammer, both. If   we forgave ourselves for making
What we have made, we would destroy what we have made
Before we'd let ourselves enjoy it, no, we won't
Release ourselves to joy with our forgiveness, never
And so we build a tower from the top of which
We hope to reach forgiveness.   Opportunities
For one to be unhappy are unlimited
A pitch of silence in the everyday unsounding
One's opportunities   belong to one, but rogue
Unhappinesses claim their midsts in a consuming
Infinity that even now approaches yours
As Enya did it, though you didn't notice.   Listen
The songs are hits, but listening, the sure connections
Between all things become long clouds.   America
The sure connections fray in clouds at the Capitol
And those who scream they want you back have never seen you
And wouldn't recognize you if you came,   and those
Who lie facedown on the floor in the chamber see the floor
Only. The woman   on the other side of the door
Wide-eyed and bleeding, sees no metaphors. O music
Where have you fled? O music, who will make you new

AFTERHEX 1

One's opportunities to be unhappy are
Dynamic, ever-expanding, a Ford Mustang chasing
The sun as it sprints panicked to the western limit
Which is the first day you don't think of the insurrection

And for weeks afterward,   and following what once
Had seemed, and anybody   would have said so, seemed to
Have been a sequence of events in time, and only
To the intelligentsia, then hidden, now

They scurry from one nimbus to another down
The block until they disappear in darkness, then
They reappear in light, then disappear again
In darkness,   and then finally beneath the next

Streetlight they're gone,   they disappear in light, to whom
What seemed to you a sequence was a sphere of time
Expanding in a space with limits, and with walls at
Its limits, in which objects are a tax the space pays

To what authority? The sphere of the riot, for
What seemed like weeks, but it was only minutes, the
Sphere was conveyed, a polished   gem, from hand to hand
One representative to the next, one party to

The other, in the weeks of their competitive
Expressions of concern, in the minutes of those weeks
Rolling, a golden coin across scarred knuckles, a
Magician or a criminal, but both, the coin

A sphere in the space between two hands, a coin in the hand
Eventually, like bullets in America
The riot passes through our heads and we forget
The riot, everything, what once seemed strange to you

Becomes your heart, American, your heart's blood strange
To you, hidden in you, the truest part of you
Unknowable, a minotaur of the hidden god
Who is not you, the god, not even of your own heart

AFTERHEX 3

One's opportunities to be unhappy are
One's singlemost inheritance, all other un
-ities requiring acknowledgment of pen
-dant interests, it's a miracle to whom, what person
You're still alive?   The city is an alphabet
Of numbers, those past 26 a sudden never
-Ending and boundlessness, but once so short and narrow
You sang it as you smashed toy trains together, the
Sneering green engine smashing into the blue engine
That really smiled, how useful, but how really useful
Reverse nostalgia of the unfamiliar grid
Becoming home, all comfort is decay,   the city
You're sure is not a living thing because it gets
Harder as it decays, more fatal where there's less
Of it, until it's gone and all at once not fatal
In hills you once imagined, green hills cushion-soft
Upon which you imagined you would lay a gingham
Blanket, a wicker basket, then from the latter pull
A cartoon sandwich and a cartoon slice of pie
On a white plate, life a cartoon, the world, except

The slice itself is plastic, a dog's chew toy, *your*
Dog's toy, it matches neither world exactly, not
The cartoon world you when you were a child imagined
And not the world, the wrong   colors in the cartoon
The texture of the colors wrong, no life in the world
No life at all, but in the cartoon it's too much
Of the world and all the life in the world, the plastic pie
All comfort is decay.   And you have spent your middled
Life searching for the turkey leg the greedy wolf
Pulled last from the basket in the cartoon, after watching
Which your imagination then developed almost
Without your input, you've searched   passively, it's true
You've sat at the dining table in the afternoon
And who are they, this family, you want to say
Arisen, but you want to say *They manifested*
Like moaning spirits in a bog, uncertain where
You got the image from, every Thanksgiving you
Have sat   at the festooned table in the afternoon, a bib
From the Red Lobster in the heart   of the next town over
Around your neck, knife in one hand, fork in the other
And licked your maw exactly like the greedy wolf
As if your hunger were a spell you cast on the food
But never has the cartoon turkey leg appeared
The perfect, brazen turkey leg you've hungered for
Since you were small, when you first saw the brazen leg
Drawn steaming from the picnic basket like a sword
Drawn steaming from the entrails of your enemy

THE DEAD NEGRO IN THE
MODERNIST LONG POEM

To decorate your poems with our deaths
Bodies of rivers being black flesh in water
And bones in flesh, loosed   from the threatening muscles
        Unknowable as laughter

In rooms in which the laughter stops   the moment
You enter,   where the faces are all faces
Of who will soon be dead, although they live
        Dead in a poem, and faceless

Hanging from the tree of knowledge   at the source
Poet, of your childhood shame, of the branchéd river
It is a hanging tree where it begins
        Of which you are the flower

IN THE EVENT OF

Officer how you know I'm dancing is the body
-cam. Look, I'm riding centuries of whips, the first half

Of the ghost, arms out the window up, the second half
Arms flat on the pavement, palms down, now the ghost is whole

My arms stretched forward, like I'm bowing, but if I
Were standing, stretched above my head. Officer how

You know I'm dead is that I seem to bow to you

NOTE

"The Phantom Son" is for G. C. Waldrep.

ACKNOWLEDGMENTS

Thank you, always, to Timothy Donnelly, Sasha Dugdale, Jonathan Galassi, Alan Gilbert, Derek Gromadski, Anastasios Karnazes, Dorothea Lasky, Melissa McCrae, Joshua Mehigan, Bradford Morrow, Paul Muldoon, Deborah Paredez, James K. A. Smith, G. C. Waldrep, and Lynn Xu for their friendship and encouragement and support. And thank you to the editors and staffs of the following journals, in which earlier versions of the following poems first appeared:

Bad Lilies: "As If Its Prison," "I Have Mixed My Labor with the Soil," and "The Many Hundreds of the Scent"

bath magg: "In the House from Which I Was Kidnapped"

Conjunctions: "Hex," "Ode," "Seagulls Crying," "The Speech of the Thin King's Minder," and "The Staggering Man"

The Hampden-Sydney Poetry Review: "Helen"

jubilat: "Race in the Body" and "Race in Language"

The New York Review of Books: "In the Ditch Where the Camera Finds My Body"

Ploughshares: "Your Black Child"

PN Review: "Reading Is on Your List of Chores"

The Poetry Review: "The Dead Negro in the Modernist Long Poem," "Explaining My Appearance in Certain Pictures," "Far Past the End," and "The Fungus Called Dead Man's Fingers"

"In the Event Of" was originally published as part of the Academy of American Poets' Poem-a-Day project.

"Hex," "Race in the Body," and "Race in Language" were included in a chapbook titled *Hex and Other Poems*, published by Bad Betty Press.

"Ode" and "Reading Is on Your List of Chores" were included in a chapbook titled *The Word Is Wild and Sad*, published by Theaphora Editions.